The Gingerbread Man

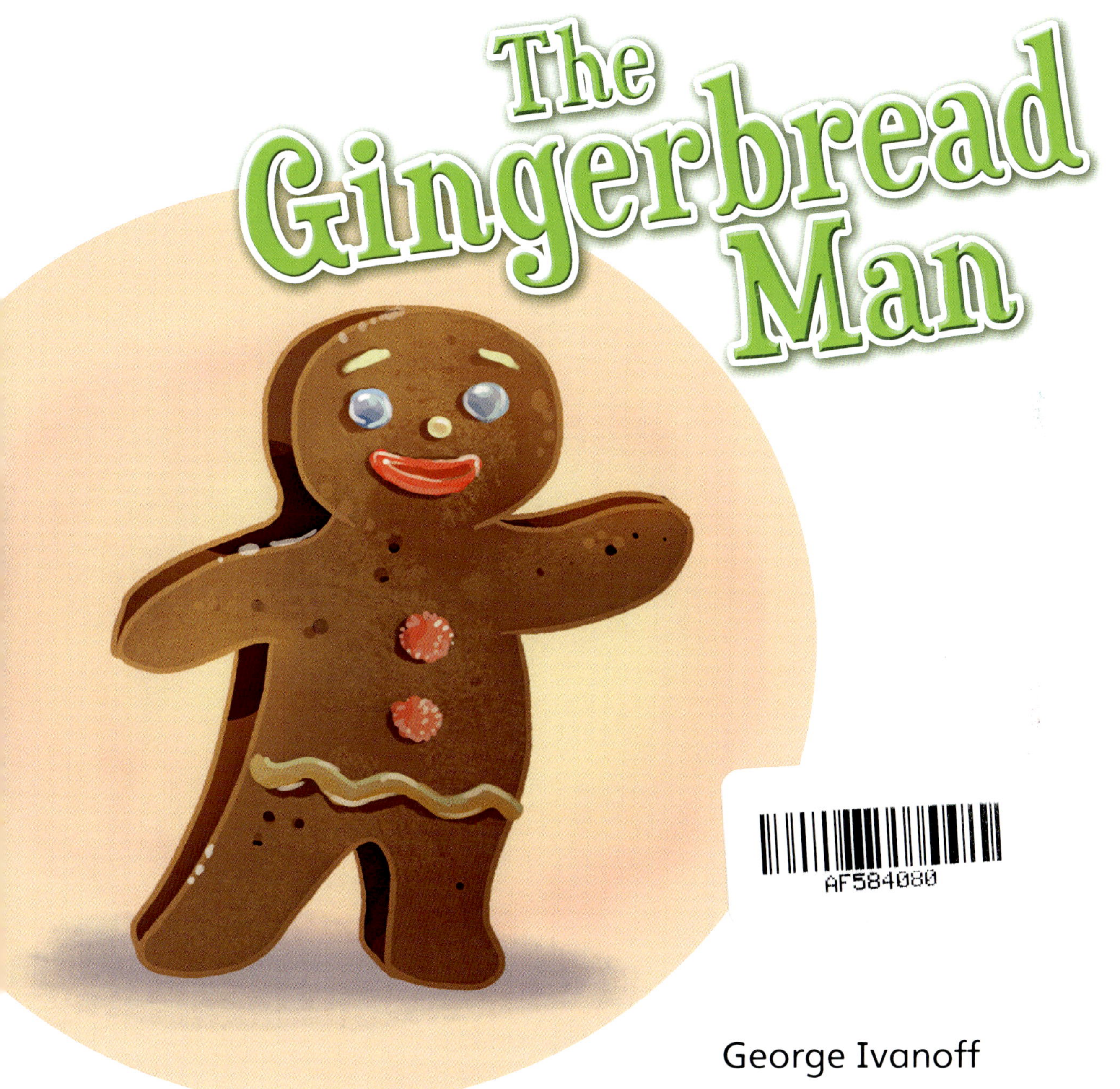

George Ivanoff

Illustrated by Diane Le Feyer

Once upon a time, there was a fairytale.
It was called 'The Gingerbread Man'.

Sarah and Joe went to the library
to read the story.
As they started to read...

…a fairy appeared!
"I am Fifi the Fairytale Fixit Fairy," she said.
"Something is wrong with this story.
Can you help me fix it?"

Fifi waved her wand.
Sarah and Joe fell through the pages
of the book and into the story.

They landed outside a cottage.
There was a gingerbread man
hopping up and down outside the door.
“Chase me!” he called.

An old woman hobbled out of the cottage.
“I can’t chase you,” she said.
“I’m too old and slow.”

An old man shuffled out of the cottage.
“I can’t chase you,” he said.
“I’m too tired and grumpy.”

“But you have to chase the gingerbread man,” said Sarah. “Or there won’t be a story.”
Fifi nodded.

The man and woman shook their heads.
"We can't do it!" they said.

“What can we do?” asked Joe.
Sarah scratched her head and thought.

“When I need to get somewhere quickly,” said Sarah, “I use a scooter.”
“Where do we get one?” asked Joe.

Sarah looked at Fifi.
“Can you get a scooter or two?” she asked.
“Of course I can,” said Fifi, waving her wand.

Two scooters appeared.
The man got on one of the scooters and tried it out.
"Hey, this is fun!" he said.

The woman got on the other scooter.
They both looked at the gingerbread man
and grinned hungrily.
The gingerbread man ran off.

“Thank you for fixing the story,” said Fifi. “Now, let’s go home.”

“Can’t we chase the gingerbread man too?” asked Joe. “I think I’d like a bite!”